Life's
Little Handbook
of
Wisdom

Member of the
Evangelical Christian
Publishers Association

Published by   Barbour and Company, Inc.
              P.O. Box 719
              Uhrichsville, Ohio 44683

Printed in the United States of America

Life's
Little Handbook
of
Wisdom

Bruce and Cheryl Bickel
Stan and Karin Jantz

A BARBOUR BOOK

Meet the Lord every morning.

Have a passion for God and compassion for people.

Choose the way of most persistence rather
than the path of least resistance.

What happens *in* you is more important than what
happens *to* you.

Seek out quiet people. They have a lot
to say if you say something first.

Celebrate spiritual birthdays. If you don't know yours, arbitrarily select a date.

———※———

It is never too late to make a change in your life.

———※———

Pray for people you dislike.

———※———

Pray for people who dislike you.

———※———

Prosperity is not always good, and adversity is not always bad.

If what you are doing won't make a difference in five years, it probably doesn't matter now.

———❦———

Develop your vocabulary, but don't overuse fancy words.

———❦———

Learn to laugh at yourself.

———❦———

Fly the flag on patriotic days.

———❦———

Pray for your family every day.

Take your kids out for ice cream after they've
performed in sports, drama, or music,
especially if they didn't do very well.

If you can't afford it, you don't need it.

Learn to tell a good story.

Live life on purpose, not by accident.

Read *How to Win Friends and Influence People*
by Dale Carnegie at least once a year.

Rent movies you could watch with your
mother in the room.

———❦———

Encourage others to develop their
character by displaying yours.

———❦———

Let your word be your bond:
keep your promises;
meet your deadlines;
honor your commitments;
pay your bills.

———❦———

Expect Christ's return.

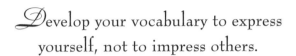

*D*evelop your vocabulary to express
yourself, not to impress others.

———◆———

*D*on't complain about the mud
if you prayed for rain.

———◆———

*R*ent classic romance and comedy videos.

———◆———

*S*ay "I love you" to your spouse at least once a day.
Say it all the time with your eyes.

———◆———

*P*ray with perseverance and expectancy.

You'll know when something becomes meaningful
to you when it goes from your head to
your heart to your hands.

Check the batteries in your smoke detector. Now.

Watch an epic Bible movie with your family
every year during Easter week.

Don't wait for memories to happen.
Plan them in advance.

Enjoy happiness; treasure joy.

*D*on't be obsessed with your weight.
Good health is much more important
than a single-digit dress size.

---

*B*efore you begin an extended car trip with your
family, take a moment to pray together for safety.

---

*P*ut loose change in a jar and save it.

---

*D*ecide, on a daily basis, not to complain.

---

*P*lant a tree to commemorate a significant event.
It will serve as a great reminder in future years.

Never let your yearning exceed your earnings.

———❦———

Expose your children to live theater or the symphony.
They'll enjoy it now and appreciate it later.

———❦———

Remember that God values you for
who you are, not *what* you do.

———❦———

You will have no greater joy than to hear
that your children walk in truth.

———❦———

The difference between mediocre and excellent is
usually a very small amount of effort.

Discover your spiritual gifts. Then, get involved
in a ministry so you can use them.

If you want to be rich—give.

If you want to be poor—grasp.

If you want abundance—scatter.

If you want to be needy—hoard.

Be loyal to your
spouse. Express
admiration
in public.

Use a credit card only if you can pay the bill
in full at the end of the month.

———❧———

Be one who says positive things about others.

———❧———

Read one book a month.

———❧———

Reward your kids every time they read
a book; even if it's for school.

———❧———

It has never been too long to renew an old friendship.

In every situation, ask yourself,
"What would Jesus do?" Then do it.

───※───

Ask for advice often. Offer advice sparingly.

───※───

Let your difficulties be opportunities
for God's control.

───※───

Compliment your spouse with elegant words.

───※───

Teach your kids responsibility early.

*N*ever mistake activity for achievement.

———❀———

*T*ake the blame for your mistakes. Give
God the credit for your successes.

———❀———

*H*eed the advice you give to others.

———❀———

*B*efore you worry needlessly, ask yourself, "What's
the worst thing that could happen?"

———❀———

*C*all your mother-in-law. Tell her how much you
appreciate the person you married.

Develop an ear for music and an eye for art.

Be a peacemaker.

Take your kids to lunch on a regular basis.

When you feel like settling for less than the best,
think about what God wants for you.

Make sure your decisions are based on pure motives.

When you have the choice between taking an escalator or the stairs, take the stairs.

———

If you don't have a Bible, get one.

———

If you've got a Bible, read it.

———

If you read the Bible, believe it.

———

If you believe the Bible, live it.

It's more important to listen to another person's point of view than to express your own.

———❧———

Don't waste your time trying to be like somebody else. Only they can do that.

———❧———

Be happy for others in their good fortune.

———❧———

Criticism and finding fault are not spiritual gifts.

———❧———

The line can often be busy when conscience wishes to speak.

*D*on't be so involved in the "when"
that you miss the "now."

———◆———

*I*f you say you'll do it, DO IT!

———◆———

*F*ollow the promptings of your heart rather
than the desires of your flesh.

———◆———

*D*on't be intimidated by your peers.
God in you is always a majority.

———◆———

*M*otivate, don't denigrate.

If you have to ask if something is
right, it probably isn't.

———

What the world sees we are, they
consider Christ to be.

———

The best time to relax is when you're too busy.

———

The person who does not read good books has no
advantage over the one who can't read them.

———

Develop a unique style.

Don't make plans and then ask for the
Lord's approval. Ask the Lord to
direct your planning.

———

If what you believe doesn't affect how
you live, then it isn't very important.

———

Religion is man's attempt to find God. The Gospel
is God's place to reach man. Don't let religion
stand in the way of your salvation.

———

You will never please everyone all
of the time. Don't even try.

It's better to give your children experiences than things.

Appreciate criticism. The comment may not hit the bull's-eye, but it will probably be on target.

———❦———

Be flexible.

———❦———

If you want to go to sleep with a clear conscience, either live with integrity every day, or pray for forgiveness every night.

———❦———

Look people in the eye when you talk to them.

———❦———

Appreciate the differences in people you know. That's usually why you like them.

*L*ittle is much if God is in it.

---

*S*upport a missionary financially.

---

*G*od is more likely to speak to you with a gentle whisper than with a loud voice.

---

*L*ove is saying "no" when it's easier to say "yes."

---

*W*hen you feel insignificant, remember how important you are to God.

*W*hen you say you will pray for someone, DO IT.

---

*Y*ou are responsible for the depth of your spiritual understanding. God is responsible for the breadth of your ministry.

---

*L*ove God, not godliness.

---

*P*lan one romantic getaway a year with your spouse.

---

*L*eave enthusiastic messages on answering machines and voice mail.

Think about your question before you ask it.

———❧———

Don't be afraid to try something you don't think
you can do. You may surprise yourself and
you'll probably enjoy it.

———❧———

Find your self worth in God's unconditional love
for you, not in your accomplishments.

———❧———

If you do something wrong, admit it.

———❧———

Learn to write fascinating letters.

Remember that God's will is not so much a function
of time and place as it is an attitude of the heart.

⸺✦⸺

God will never send a thirsty soul to a dry well.

⸺✦⸺

Character is made by what you stand for;
reputation by what you fall for.

⸺✦⸺

If you want people to think that you are interesting,
ask them questions about themselves.

⸺✦⸺

From every dollar you earn save
some and tithe some.

Send cards and notes to your grandparents on special occasions, and be sure to include current pictures of the family.

Nothing is ever too small a thing to do when it is done for someone else.

Satan can't make you an unbeliever, but he'll try to make you an ineffective believer.

Have someone over on the spur of the moment.

Plan to be spontaneous.

*C*arry a spare tire (in your car trunk,
not around your waist).

———❦———

*G*ive the gift of time. It's a gift more
valuable than money can buy.

———❦———

*B*e as enthusiastic to stay married as
you were to get married.

———❦———

*D*irection is more important than speed.

———❦———

*R*emember, there is a time for love and a place
for love. Any time, any place.

Strive to be a person of faith rather than one of fame.

―――•―――

True communication begins when two
people pray together.

―――•―――

Make it a goal always to make good on your
promises, no matter how long it takes.

―――•―――

Read at least one biography a year.

―――•―――

Keep fresh flowers in your home.

*B*e a person of principle, passion, and purity.

———————

*M*ake an appointment with God every day and then
keep it as if you were meeting with the most
important person in the world.

———————

*S*atisfaction begins when comparison stops.

———————

*W*henever you feel insignificant, remember
how important you are to God.

———————

*I*f faced with a "take it or leave it"
decision, you better leave it.

Focus on your abilities rather than your limitations.

If you want to be known as a trustworthy person,
consistently back your words with action.

———

Memorize the names of the Seven Dwarfs.

———

You can still be a role model even if you're
less than a model parent.

———

Make your home a place where your
kids can bring their friends.

———

There are those who dream, and those who do, and
those who do both. Join the third group.

Feeling good about yourself begins
with serving others.

———

God will either protect you from hardship or give you
the strength to go through it. You win either way.

———

For once, resist navy blue.

———

Hold on to friendships tightly;
release possession easily.

———

Keep a guest book in your home.

God's anger lasts only a moment, but
His favor lasts a lifetime.

———

Live independently of people's opinions of you.

———

Life is too short to buy green bananas.

———

Underpromise and overdeliver.

———

Avoid making statements that can
be taken two ways.

$\mathcal{D}$o not pretend to know when all
you can offer is a guess.

$\mathcal{F}$ailing to respond to a negative comment about
someone else implies your agreement.

$\mathcal{K}$now what God expects of you. If you don't
know, look it up in the Bible.

$\mathcal{H}$umility grows out of strength. Pride
grows out of weakness.

*Y*ou will begin to live when you lose yourself
in God's purpose for you.

---

*S*pend more of your time, energy, and
resources investing in people
than you do investing in things.

---

*B*e quick to receive the truth, and even
quicker to dismiss gossip.

---

*G*enerosity does not include giving away
something you'll never miss.

Sometime in the next month, try giving the Lord
a day out of your life. An entire day.

If you maintain important relationships, they're
less likely to require repairs.

Be aware of your own body language when
listening or speaking.

If you're going to compare yourself to anyone,
compare yourself to Christ. It will put
your life in perspective.

True love is more an act of your will than
a product of your emotions.

⁂

Buy a new Christmas recording each year.

⁂

Call your pastor and tell him how
much you appreciate him.

⁂

Commit yourself to projects; dedicate
yourself to people.

⁂

Take the family camping at least once a year.

Keep a family photo album up to date.

———

Rejoice in the Lord's discipline
as well as in His blessings.

———

Listen to books on tape when you
take extended car trips.

———

Make a daily habit of reading the chapter in Proverbs
that corresponds to the current date.

———

Roast marshmallows over a campfire.

*F*aith is not an emotion. It is objective trust
placed in a very real God.

———

*I*f you want to know what's in your heart,
listen to your mouth.

———

*W*hen you develop your film, get double prints.
Give the duplicates away.

———

*G*od won't take away a sin until you
give it over to Him.

———

*P*eople are attracted to enthusiasm.

Make your
home a place
where people feel
welcome.

*D*on't be afraid to ask.

———

*H*ave your next goal in mind before you achieve
the one you are working on.

———

*A*s a Christian, you are designed and equipped to
change the world for God's glory.

———

*Y*ou learn more by listening. (You already
know what you would say.)

———

*F*eeling sorry for someone is okay;
helping them is better.

$\mathcal{A}$ decision may not get easier with delay.

$\mathcal{M}$anage your money as if it belongs to God. It does.

$\mathcal{K}$now when to choose between giving someone a pat on the back or a kick in the pants.

$\mathcal{K}$eep a selection of greeting cards on hand so you'll have one on the spur of the moment.

$\mathcal{W}$henever possible, word your criticism in the form of a challenge.

Take out the trash before the garbage
truck is two houses away.

———

It is hard to learn from a mistake you
don't acknowledge making.

———

If you agree to bury the hatchet, don't
leave the handle sticking out.

———

Thank God that your salvation does
not depend on you.

If doctrine is your motivation, you will be a
fanatic; if God is your motivation,
you will be an obedient servant.

———

Understand the difference between acting
young and being immature.

———

The parents' role is not to make all the right choices
for their children, but to teach them how
to make those choices for themselves.

———

Have a best friend who can multiply your
joy and divide your sorrow.

We can't always choose the situations that life
brings us, but we can choose the attitudes
we will use to face them.

———

Always leave the campsite cleaner than you found it.

———

A modest person may not be noticed at
first but will be respected later.

———

Never be ashamed of your faith.

———

You'll miss your opportunities if you're too
busy looking for a sure thing.

A card sent with a personal note inside is so much more meaningful than a card sent but only signed.

Ask the Lord to teach you His ways.

The person who often looks up to God rarely looks down on anyone.

Visit the Holy Land one time in your life.

Remember those who are alone, especially on holidays.

Give your spouse a gift for no reason.

———❧———

Learn to read music.

———❧———

Dine by candlelight at least once a week.

———❧———

Our five senses are incomplete without the sixth—a sense of humor.

———❧———

Enjoy the journey as much as the destination.

———❧———

Love is forgiving and for giving.

Plant some bulbs in your garden. You'll enjoy
the flowers year after year.

⁓

Read the front page of a local newspaper every day.
Keep up with current events.

⁓

When you travel, eat in local restaurants.

⁓

Instead of bringing your kids presents after
a business trip, give them your time.

⁓

Always try to see the forest through the trees.

*D*evelop priorities.

※

*W*rite down the name of your closest friend in the world. Now pick up a phone and place a call.

※

*Y*ou don't need a house to have a home.

※

*R*emember, people don't look as critically at you as you look at yourself.

※

*C*ompliment people as soon as it occurs to you.

Do something for someone without taking credit.

*W*hen you're feeling overwhelmed, make a list.

---

*D*o the job assigned to you with excellence,
and opportunity will find you.

---

*B*e efficient, but don't cut corners.

A word spoken in anger cannot be erased.
It plays over and over again.

---

*L*earn about nutrition: feed your body healthy foods.

If you don't stand for something,
you'll fall for anything.

———❦———

A testimony is better than a title.

———❦———

Be cautious in telling others what you can do, but
be bold in asserting what God can do.

———❦———

If you want to build a life of spiritual leadership,
begin with a foundation of prayer.

———❦———

Discipline begins with small things done daily.

Instead of valuing something by its cost,
figure out how much it's worth.

———❦———

Once in a while, set a goal that absolutely scares you.

———❦———

Make it your constant goal to be
obedient, not victorious.

———❦———

Recognition is good; admiration is better.

———❦———

On a rainy day show your kids their baby pictures.

If you want to lead, read.

Learn to relax without feeling guilty.

Write a thank-you note to a Sunday school
teacher from your past.

Don't worry so much about where you *are*
as where you are *going*.

You should always believe what you say, but you
don't always need to say what you think.

*G*ive thanks before each meal.

———❦———

*H*ave a ready smile and a firm handshake.

———❦———

*L*earn from the mistakes of others. You'll never live long enough to make them all yourself.

———❦———

*R*ead for fifteen minutes every night before you go to bed.

———❦———

*D*evelop your own abilities while discovering the abilities of others.

*L*isten with your eyes as well as with your ears.

———

*L*earn to thrive on challenge and change.

———

*M*ake sure your caring includes doing.

———

*L*earn the proper names of the trees in your yard.

———

*M*ake moments of stillness, quiet, and solitude
part of your daily routine.